EVENTS & OUTCOMES
THE
INDUSTRIAL
REVOLUTION

NIGEL SMITH

RAINTREE
STECK-VAUGHN
PUBLISHERS

A Harcourt Company

Austin   New York
www.raintreesteckvaughn.com

First published 2003 by Raintree Steck-Vaughn
Publishers, an imprint of Steck-Vaughn Company

© Evans Brothers Limited 2002

Library of Congress Cataloging-in-Publication Data
is available upon request

ISBN 0-7398-5799-1

Printed in Spain. Bound in the United States.

1 2 3 4 5 6 7 8 9 0 LB 05 04 03 02

Edited by Rachel Norridge
Designed by Neil Sayer
Consultant: Professor Eric Hopkins

Acknowledgments

Cover image the art archive; **background image** Mary Evans Picture Library; **p. 6** (top) Peter
Newark's American Pictures, (bottom) The Bridgeman Art Library; **p. 7** The Bridgeman Art Library;
p. 8 The Bridgeman Art Library; **p. 9** (top) Topham Picturepoint, (bottom) Bridgeman Art Library;
p. 10 The Bridgeman Art Library; **p. 11** Mary Evans Picture Library; **p. 12** The Bridgeman Art
Library; **p. 13** Mary Evans Picture Library; **p. 14** The Bridgeman Art Library; **p. 15** The Bridgeman
Art Library; **p. 16** Mary Evans Picture Library; **p. 17** The Bridgeman Art Library; **p. 18** The Bridgeman
Art Library; **p. 19** the art archive; **p. 20** Mary Evans Picture Library; **p. 21** Mary Evans Picture
Library; **p. 22** The Bridgeman Art Library; **p. 23** (top) art archive, (bottom) Mary Evans Picture
Library; **p. 24** The Bridgeman Art Library; **p. 25** (top) Topham Picturepoint, (bottom) the art archive;
p. 26 the art archive; **p. 27** Mary Evans Picture Library; **p. 29** (top) the art archive, (bottom) Mary
Evans Picture Library; **p. 30** Mary Evans Picture Library; **p. 31** Mary Evans Picture Library; **p. 32**
(top) Topham Picturepoint, (bottom) the art archive; **p. 33** Topham Picturepoint; **p. 34** Mary Evans
Picture Library; **p. 35** Mary Evans Picture Library; **p. 36** Mary Evans Picture Library; **p. 37** the art
archive; **p. 38** The Bridgeman Art Library; **p. 39** (top) Mary Evans Picture Library, (bottom) the art
archive; **p. 40** (top) Topham Picturepoint, (bottom) Mary Evans Picture Library; **p. 41** (left) Mary
Evans Picture Library, (right) The Bridgeman Art Library; **p. 42** the art archive; **p. 43** Mary Evans
Picture Library; **p. 44** Mary Evans Picture Library; **p. 45** Mary Evans Picture Library; **p. 46** Mary
Evans Picture Library; **p. 47** (top) the art archive, (bottom) Mary Evans Picture Library; **p. 48** Mary
Evans Picture Library; **p. 49** (top) the art archive, (bottom) Mary Evans Picture Library; **p. 50** Mary
Evans Picture Library; **p. 51** The Bridgeman Art Library; **p. 52** Mary Evans Picture Library; **p. 53**
(top) The Bridgeman Art Library, (bottom) Topham Picturepoint; **p. 54** The Bridgeman Art Library;
p. 55 (top) Mary Evans Picture Library, (bottom) the art archive; **p. 56** (top) Mary Evans Picture
Library, (bottom) Mary Evans Picture Library; **p. 57** the art archive; **p. 58** The Bridgeman Art
Library; **p. 59** Metropolitan Borough of Rochdale Community Services Dept.; **p. 60** The Bridgeman
Art Library; **p. 61** Topham Picturepoint; **p. 62** Mary Evans Picture Library; **p. 63** Mary Evans
Picture Library; **p. 64** (top) Mary Evans Picture Library; **p. 65** (top) The Bridgeman Art Library,
(bottom) Mary Evans Picture Library; **p. 66** Mary Evans Picture Library; **p. 67** (top) the art archive,
(bottom) Mary Evans Picture Library; **p. 68** the art archive; **p. 69** (top) Mary Evans Picture Library,
(bottom) the art archive; **p. 70** the art archive; **p .71** (top) the art archive, (bottom) The Bridgeman
Art Library; **p. 72** Mary Evans Picture Library

CONTENTS

A DIFFERENT REVOLUTION

The surrender of British General Burgoyne at Saratoga in 1777 was the turning point in the American Revolution.

The late 18th century was an age of revolutions. For many people, it was a period of change and uncertainty. In the United States, the colonists had seized their independence from Great Britain in the revolutionary war of 1775–1783. In France, the Revolution of 1789 had overthrown the monarchy and terrified royal families and rulers all over Europe. Revolutionary ideas, embracing the rights of the common man and rejecting the privileges of a few, were eagerly discussed in many countries by those who wanted to create a fairer society. In spite of the enthusiasm of a few British radicals, there was never any real possibility of a political revolution in Britain. Instead, by the 1780s, a different kind of revolution was beginning.

The phrase "Industrial Revolution" describes the development of a nation's economy from one based on small-scale manufacture in cottages and workshops to one founded on large-scale, factory-based industries. It also brings about a change from a rural-based society, in which most people live and work on the land, to an urban society where most people live and work in towns and cities. Industrial growth also usually gives rise to wealthy entrepreneurs accumulating profits and reinvesting them.

Only a few 18th-century farmers could afford to use machinery.

First Industrial Nation

Great Britain was the world's first industrial nation. From the 1780s, the pace of industrialization quickened and, in many different ways, altered an entire way of life for millions of people. By 1850, Britain had been transformed. Even its physical appearance had changed —new factory towns blighted the landscape with their countless chimneys pouring out smoke, and busy railway lines threaded across the country creating a network of industrial towns. The Industrial Revolution converted Britain from a small, rural nation into the wealthiest and most powerful country in the world.

Was It a Revolution?

When we speak of revolution, we usually refer to great changes taking place over a fairly short space of time. Britain was the first country to experience these great industrial changes. Yet some historians have questioned whether the "Industrial Revolution" was really a revolution. The roots of industrialization go back at least a century, and the process of industrialization took about a hundred years before it could be described as virtually complete.

Louis Blanqui (1805–1881), a French politician who supported the ideas of the French Revolution, appears to have first used the term "Industrial Revolution." Blanqui wrote that the economic changes that Britain experienced were just as important as the political changes that had altered French life in 1789. Just as the events in France had an influence far beyond France's borders, so Britain's Industrial Revolution affected Germany, Italy, the United States, and eventually Russia.

West Hartlepool, England, in 1859—a new industrial town that owed its growth to the railways and the iron and steel industry.

Progress for the People?

Historians also question the extent to which industrialization benefited the majority of people at the time. In 1750, most people were poor. According to Joseph Massie, a contemporary economist, the bottom 40 percent of the population existed on less than 14 percent of the country's income. Some historians argue that while there were improvements in living standards for the middle and upper classes, plus benefits for the working class such as cheaper food and clothes and later cheaper train travel, these benefits were more than cancelled out by the poor housing and working conditions that accompanied industrial progress and growth.

A Growing Nation

New methods of selective breeding increased the weight of animals and reduced the price of meat.

On the eve of the Industrial Revolution, most people in Britain lived south of a line from East Anglia to the Bristol Channel. Since the 1600s, the population had been growing at an ever-increasing rate. From approximately 5.5 million in 1700 to 5.8 million in 1750, the population then jumped to 9 million in 1801—a rise of 39 percent between 1750 and 1801.

Plagues, such as the bubonic plague that had killed large numbers of people in 1665, had been eliminated with the unexplained disappearance of the plague-carrying black rat. Beginning in the 1770s, agricultural changes and good harvests reduced the price of food; this benefitted childbearing women, who were better able to rear healthy children. At the same time, the birthrate was rising, people seemed to be marrying younger, and family size was increasing. In 1700, the average age of marriage for a woman was 26. By 1800, it had fallen to 23, while the proportion of women who did not marry decreased by more than 50 percent.

Some people were alarmed at this sudden increase in the population. They argued that if it continued, food shortages would result. The British Reverend Thomas Malthus (1766–1834) forecast that there would eventually be a famine. In his *Essay on the Principle of Population* (1798), he said:

It may safely be pronounced that population, when unchecked, goes on doubling itself every twenty-five years. Considering the present average state of the earth, the means of subsistence could not possibly be made to increase this quickly.

Thomas Malthus was, however, proven wrong. The growth of population went hand in hand with the Industrial Revolution and accompanying improvements in agriculture. Industrial and agricultural progress made it possible to support an increasing population. In fact, population growth was essential to the Industrial Revolution in providing an enlarged workforce and a growing base of customers. The biggest incentive to entrepreneurs to pursue industrialization was the knowledge that they could easily sell their products because the markets for them were constantly expanding.

Thomas Malthus warned of disaster if the world's population continued to grow.

Managing Change

Before the Industrial Revolution, the pace and way of life scarcely changed during most people's lives. Yet those who lived during any part of the Industrial Revolution lived through greater changes than had any of their ancestors. Some people usually suffer because of change —for example, when new methods of production lead to job losses. Today, people are used to rapid change whether it is in technology, fashion and design, or even in the food they eat. An important task for modern-day government is to manage change so that benefit is maximized and discomfort and hardship kept to a minimum. However, during the Industrial Revolution, governments were firmly opposed to any measure that might be perceived as interference with industry. Entrepreneurs were free to run their businesses exactly as they chose.

Industrialization created a new social group—the working class —who worked and lived together in the new factory towns.

1750: INDUSTRY ON THE BRINK OF CHANGE

The Domestic System

In 1750, most people lived and worked in rural areas and agriculture was Great Britain's main industry. Closely linked to farming was Britain's largest manufacturing industry—the woolen industry. Wool cloth had an international market and was an important export. In the West Country, East Anglia, and the West Riding of Yorkshire, it had been manufactured for centuries in the domestic system. Entire families worked in their cottages producing cloth with only simple tools and machines. Businessmen, known as clothiers, organized production. The raw wool was delivered to the cottages and the finished product collected. In the cottages, women usually did the spinning while men weaved the woolen thread into cloth.

Domestic workers enjoyed some independence but worked long hours to make a living.

Although the domestic system was only able to produce quite small amounts of cloth, it was reasonably adequate for the needs of the population before 1750. Working in the domestic system had definite advantages. Domestic workers could still look after their children and did not have to travel any distance to work. They could also perhaps grow food or keep livestock on a small farm. On the other hand, people had to work very long hours to make a living, often in small, cramped spaces. In 1724, Daniel Defoe wrote of the domestic system:

Within we saw the houses full of lusty fellows … the people in general live long; they enjoy a good air. Under such circumstances hard labor is naturally attended with the blessing of health, if not riches.

Yet this is an idealized account—such conditions were not as perfect as they might have seemed.

King Cotton

The cotton gin made many white plantation owners in the U.S. South very wealthy.

By 1850, three million slaves worked on the U.S. plantations. The contentious issue of slavery was not addressed fully until the terrible Civil War, 1861–1865.

Cotton had many advantages over wool. Cotton clothing was lighter and softer to wear. It could be washed more easily and so was more hygienic—an important consideration when domestic dwellings did not have supplies of running water. At first, cotton was expensive, but by the late 18th century supplies were increasing. Moreover, the price was falling because it was produced by slave labor in the West Indies and the United States.

In 1793, a young American named Eli Whitney revolutionized cotton production with his invention of the cotton gin. It was the most important invention made in the U.S. up to that time. Until then, cotton was separated from its seeds by hand. One person working all day could only separate less than one pound (half a kilogram) of cotton. Whitney's gin (short for "engine") could separate over 1,000 pounds (455 kilograms) in a day. His invention made cotton growing in the Southern states extremely profitable, with most of the exports going to Britain to be manufactured into cloth (the American South preferred to ship raw cotton elsewhere, instead of producing textiles locally). In 1792, the South exported 76 tons of cotton, but by 1800 the amount had risen to 8,637 tons, and was rising. "Cotton," the white Southerners said, "is king."

In 1800, there were only about five million Americans, including 880,000 slaves, and most cotton was grown for export. But the boom in cotton stimulated the rise of American textile mills and by 1810 there were 87 mills, most of them in the New England states.

A negative effect of Whitney's invention was the increase in the use of black slaves and, with it, the determination of the South to stick to slavery in spite of opposition from the Northern states.

Cotton trade with the United States made Liverpool Britain's busiest port. In 1838, the first transatlantic steamer service further increased the port's importance.

The Lancashire Cotton Industry

The availability of this cheap cotton brought great benefits to the British cotton industry. By 1812, it had overtaken wool as the major textile industry. Lancashire, with its great port of Liverpool, was its center, with raw cotton from the U.S. arriving at this port. Imports of raw cotton were growing fast.

Imports of Raw Cotton Per Decade	
	millions of pounds
1750–59	2.86 (1.3 kg)
1760–69	3.53 (1.6 kg)
1770–79	5.07 (2.3 kg)
1780–89	15 (6.8 kg)
1790–99	27.6 (12.5 kg)
1800–09	57.3 (26. kg)
1810–19	92.6 (42 kg)
1820–29	165 (75 kg)
1830–39	288.8 (131 kg)
1840–49	529 (240 kg)
1850–59	7,619 (3,456 kg)

Fast streams, plentiful coal, and a fairly damp climate that helped keep the thread from breaking, all made Lancashire the ideal location for cotton mills.

The cotton industry produced great prosperity and employed thousands of people. It was also a very important export—Britain was the only country that was mass-producing manufactured cotton goods and they were exported all over the world. In 1835, E. Baines noted that:

The fabrics of cotton exported in one year would form a girdle passing eleven times round the equator. This manufacture furnishes nearly one half of British exports, and it supplies almost every nation of the world with some portion of its clothing.

The Arrival of the Factories

After 1750, the population of Britain was increasing quite rapidly and with it, the demand for clothing. Clothiers knew that if they could increase production and, at the same time, reduce costs so that cloth and clothes would be cheaper, they would make bigger profits. This was a powerful incentive for new inventions in the textile industry and gave rise to the idea of factory mass production for the first time.

One of the first key inventions was John Kay's (1704–1764) flying shuttle in 1733. Two weavers were needed to weave broadcloth, which was wider than a weaver's arms could reach. The flying shuttle used hammers to knock the shuttle back and forth and allowed a single weaver to produce broadcloth. In 1755, Jedediah Strutt (1726–1797) invented a gadget that improved the stocking frame so that ribbed stockings, which were stronger and warmer, could be made by machine instead of by hand. Strutt became extremely wealthy from his invention.

Each improvement and invention led to yet further developments. The early inventions increased the demand for thread beyond that which hand spinning could produce. James Hargreaves (d. 1778) solved the problem around 1764 with his spinning jenny. Before long, this machine could spin up to 120 threads simultaneously. This solution to the shortage of thread had an enormous impact on the textile industry. However, not everyone welcomed this new machine. Hand-spinners were frightened that the spinning jenny would replace them. In 1768, a mob of domestic spinners wrecked Hargreaves's Lancashire home and he was forced to flee.

The spinning jenny revolutionized textile production, but it was also a cause of hardship for traditional hand-spinners.

Machines and Factories

Arkwright probably got the idea for his water frame from someone else. His real skill was as a successful entrepreneur.

One of the spinning jenny's problems was that the thread it produced wasn't very strong and was liable to break. In 1775, Richard Arkwright's (1732–1792) water frame (so-called because it worked by water power) built on previous ideas to make a much stronger thread. Arkwright's neighbors nicknamed it the "Devil's Bagpipes" because of the noise it made. However, because the water frame was a large, cumbersome machine, it was not suitable for domestic production and could only be used in a factory. Arkwright became known as the "Father of the Factory System" after he built the first cotton mills to accommodate his water frames at Cromford, Derbyshire, in 1771. He employed over 300 workers in this entirely new way of producing goods. For the first time, cloth was mass-produced and, as a result, it was much cheaper. With several partners, Arkwright established a number of factories, and by 1782 he was enormously wealthy and employing more than 5,000 workers.

In 1779, a Bolton weaver, Samuel Crompton (1753–1827), made a further advance with his spinning mule. It combined the best points of the spinning jenny with the water frame. The mule made strong thread that could be used to produce high quality cloth. The final development in the transformation of the textile industry came with Edmund Cartwright's (1743–1823) power loom. Cartwright, a clergyman, had visited Arkwright's mill in 1784. Hand-weavers could not keep up with the increased production of yarn, and Cartwright saw the need for a power-driven loom to do the weaving.

Arkwright's cotton mills were the first factories in the world to use power-driven machinery. They were the beginning of the end for the domestic system of production.

Cartwright perfected his machine in 1787. At first it was driven by the weaver's feet, but by 1789 steam engines were driving the looms. Soon other entrepreneurs, recognizing the opportunity to boost profits, built factories and installed the latest machines. By 1788, there were 143 Arkwright-type mills and by 1838 there were more than 100,000 power looms being used in textile factories.

The cotton textile industry was the first to be industrialized. Cotton was called "the wonder of the age" and overtook the woolen industry in importance. The woolen industry was much slower to adopt mechanical spinning and weaving, and the domestic system continued to endure for many years. The factory system in woolen production was not complete until the 1870s.

Sir Richard Arkwright craved the lifestyle of a rich landowner. When he died, he left half a million pounds, a vast sum at the time.

Industrialization in America

Britain led the way and made great efforts to guard her secrets. Until 1843, laws restricted the export of British machinery. But secrets are hard to keep. In 1790, Samuel Slater (1768–1835), an English trained cotton-mill mechanic, emigrated to the United States and built, from memory, America's first cotton-spinning machine at Pawtucket, Rhode Island. Unwittingly, Slater had transported the industrial revolution to America.

However, America was much slower than Britain to industrialize. In the early days, most factories catered only to local needs. Some Americans subscribed to the ideas of Thomas Jefferson (1743–1826), third president of the U.S., who believed that working for wages opposed the idea of individual freedom. Proponents of this argument wanted America to remain a nation of independent farmers. This lack of competition was to Britain's advantage. In the early 19th century, no one could foresee that the United States would, many years later, overtake Britain to become the world's most important industrial nation.

Financing the Industrial Revolution

In the early years of the 18th century, very little money was needed to set up a business. However, the development of new machinery and the need to build factories meant that money had to be spent before a business could begin to make any profit. At first, the amounts needed were quite small, but as machinery became more complex it became more expensive to buy. The opportunity to make large profits encouraged wealthy individuals to invest money, known as capital, in new and expanding businesses. The greatest investment was in the cotton industry, helping the rapid spread of textile mills and cotton cloth production.

Sources of Capital

Where did this money come from? The capital needed to finance the Industrial Revolution was readily available in Britain. Some came from the profits of overseas trade, including capital from shipowners involved in the terrible but very lucrative transatlantic slave trade from West Africa to the Americas.

Much of Britain's wealth in the 18th century was in the form of land ownership. Improvements in farming

Slaves en route to America. In 1807, Parliament stopped British ships from taking part in the slave trade. The U.S. followed in 1809.

meant that land rents were rising and farming was a profitable business. Many wealthy landowners chose to invest the growing profits they made from rents and agriculture in various business ventures.

Some investment came from the profits of industry. Factory owners poured some of their increasing profits back into the business in order to maximize future returns. Jeremy Bentham (1748–1832), an English writer and philosopher, coined the word "capitalist" to describe factory owners who operated in this way.

Agricultural improvers, such as Robert Bakewell, boosted not only the profits of farming but, indirectly, those of industry, too.

The Role of Banking

The growth of banking was also essential in order for industry to flourish. From only a dozen banks in 1750, there were probably about 700 by 1815. These banks helped in the day-to-day running of businesses by dealing with payments, receiving deposits, and paying out wages. In addition, the banks gave out loans and advances, which helped factory owners to expand their operations and invest in the latest machinery.

The Royal Exchange and the Bank of England helped make London the most important financial center in the 19th century.

Why Did Britain Lead the Way?

Why did the Industrial Revolution originate in Great Britain? A number of unique advantages and circumstances made the Industrial Revolution possible there before it occurred anywhere else.

In Britain, agricultural improvements that fed more people but required fewer people to work on the land were being made simultaneously with a growth in population. This meant that there was an available workforce for the new factories as well as customers for the new products. Cash was available to purchase new machinery, and this was the incentive for inventors to apply their skills to continually improving methods of manufacture.

Britain also had a plentiful supply of water, which was used at first to drive machines in the earliest factories. The rapid expansion of overseas trade was important. Britain was a great trading nation with a considerable number of merchant ships, and it was easy and cheap to transport manufactured cloth to other countries. The availability of cheap supplies of cotton was another key ingredient for growth. Finally, there was an eagerness to experiment, to find new ways of doing things.

During the 18th century, British ships dominated international trade and British ports flourished. Bristol, shown here in 1785, profited from the slave trade and the importing of American tobacco.

Few factories would have been as agreeable as this one. Is it possible that this picture was commissioned by a factory owner?

If any of these several factors had been missing, then industrial development would have been slowed or stopped. In turn, the changes in the textile industry stimulated other industries and carried the Industrial Revolution across all industries during the 19th century. Together with coal, iron, and engineering, the textile industry provided the basis for British achievement. George Richardson Porter, a government statistician, writing in 1847, said:

 It is to the spinning-jenny and the steam engine that we must look as having been the true moving powers of our fleets and armies, and the chief support also of a long-continued agricultural prosperity.

The Work of an Elite?

Only a fairly small number of individuals pioneered the changes. A combination of bankers, investors, landowners, factory-owners, and inventors financed, organized, and presided over the early part of the Industrial Revolution. The progress that changed so much was created by a minority of people who gained a great deal for themselves. In some cases, they were acting against the wishes of the majority of people who feared that change would actually worsen their working conditions, wages, and quality of life. The revolution in the textile industry set in motion a collision of interests and fears that caused bitterness among many workers and later gave rise to a reaction against the way that they were treated. This was, perhaps, the inevitable consequence of an economic and industrial revolution.

A REVOLUTION IN POWER

Steam Power

Steam power played a large part in the Industrial Revolution; without it, industrialization would have been impossible. The most important engineering, transportation, and business developments were all connected to the steam engine. Matthew Boulton, who worked with James Watt, used the phrase,

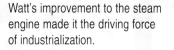

What all the world wants—power,

to describe its importance.

Before the steam engine, power was provided by human and animal energy, together with the occasional use of windmills or water mills. The domestic system used mainly hand power. The first factories were built near fast-running streams and rivers and drove machinery by water power. Water-driven machines need a constant stream of fast-flowing water. But water had many disadvantages, not least that it was unreliable and could even dry up in hot summer months. Improved machinery needed far more dependable power sources. The steam engine was the answer. Advances in steam power made further development of the Industrial Revolution possible. One of the most outstanding engineers of the time was James Watt (1736–1819), whose improvements to the steam engine were among the greatest achievements of the 18th century. They made it possible to use steam power to drive factory machinery, and later, railway locomotives and steamships.

Watt's improvement to the steam engine made it the driving force of industrialization.

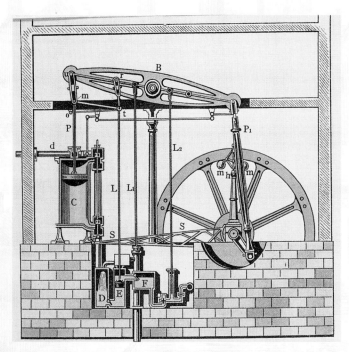

Developments in Steam

The idea of using steam power had been around since as early as the 17th century. In 1712, Thomas Savery (c.1650–1715) and Thomas Newcomen (1663–1729) both built a steam-pumping engine. These engines, known as the "Miners' Friend," were useful for pumping water out of coal mines, but had limited use elsewhere. It was not until James Watt, at the University of Glasgow, was asked to repair a working model of one of Newcomen's steam engines that real progress in steam application was made. Watt, who made and repaired various scientific instruments, realized that he could build a much better engine. Watt's engines were more powerful and used only a quarter of the coal needed by earlier engines. Yet the real breakthrough in engine design came in 1782, when Watt built a rotary engine that could turn wheels. He developed a system of gear wheels known as "sun and planet motion." For the first time, it was possible to drive textile machinery with steam power.

James Watt was an outstanding engineer of the era of industrialization. He worked closely with Matthew Boulton, a Birmingham manufacturer, to supervise the construction of his designs.

Steam Application

Steam power brought about a new way of life for those who worked in factories. Not everyone seemed to benefit from this progress.

Richard Arkwright was the first person to install one of Watt's engines to drive machines in a cotton mill. Mass production in factories was now possible, using a reliable form of power to drive spinning and weaving machines. The steam engine ensured the rapid growth of the factory system. Contemporaries were in no doubt as to its importance, as Mr. Farey wrote in the 1790s:

> *Seven hundred and fifty people work in a cotton mill, and with the help of the steam engine they will spin as much thread as 200,000 people could without any machines.... The invention of the steam engine has changed industry as the invention of gunpowder changed warfare.*

Coal Mining

Coal mining was another key industry in Britain's development. Without massive resources of coal, there would not have been an industrial revolution at all. Coal was needed to drive the steam engines, but it was also required for other industrial processes. Many industries, such as textiles and iron, were increasingly located on the coalfields. Until 1914, coal was one of Britain's main and very profitable exports.

At the start of the 18th century, coal mines were small, scattered pits, usually with no more than 30 or so miners digging from shallow, open workings. Most of the coal they dug was burned as fuel in people's homes. The most important coalfields were in Lancashire, Yorkshire, the West Midlands, the North-East of England, South Wales, and around Glasgow in Scotland. In time, as more factories were located close to coal supplies, these coalfields became the main industrial regions of Britain.

As industrial production grew and population increased, so the output of coal rose.

Growth of Coal Output 1700–1900

	millions of pounds
1700	5,600 (2,540 kg)
1750	11,197 (5,079 kg)
1800	24,636 (11,175 kg)
1825	49,270 (22,349 kg)
1850	111,980 (50,794 kg)
1870	246,354 (111,746 kg)
1900	503,904 (228,571 kg)

A pit head in about 1790. A steam-powered water pump is being used while horses and mules transport the coal.

In the 1840s, accidents were a daily occurrence in almost every mine. The government refused to force safety measures on mine owners.

Mining Safety

The extraction of all this extra coal posed many difficulties. For a start, it became necessary to mine deep into the ground to reach the rich coal seams. As mining penetrated deeper below the surface, it became more and more difficult to keep the underground shafts and tunnels free from flooding. Savery and Newcomen's steam-pumping engines helped, but it was James Watt's improved engine, first used in 1776, that was really effective for draining deep mines.

Poor ventilation and the risks of using candles or lamps underground were further problems. Many miners were killed when the buildup of dangerous gases caused massive explosions. A report of a mining disaster near Newcastle in 1769 vividly described the impact such explosions had:

One explosion was very remarkable: 70 men were blown out of the pit and a large piece of timber about ten yards long and ten inches thick was blown a considerable distance and stuck into the side of a hill.

The invention of a miners' safety lamp in 1815 by Humphrey Davy (1778–1829) made the mines safer, but even so, mining remained a very dangerous industry. From 1845 to 1867, more than 12,500 men were killed in the coal mines. One of the worst disasters occurred in 1862, when 204 miners were gassed to death at Hartley Colliery in Durham. Another cause of accidents was the frequent breakage of winching gear. The development of wire rope, first produced in 1834, helped to overcome this.

Sir Humphrey Davy, one of the greatest English chemists, made many discoveries, but is best remembered for his safety lamp.

23

A New Iron Age

Early machinery was made out of wood, but as machines became larger and more complex it was important that they were made out of stronger material such as iron or steel. Steam engines had to be constructed from iron. Fortunately, Britain had a plentiful supply of iron ore as well as the coal that was needed to turn it into iron and steel. The iron industry was important to the expansion of Britain's economy and was yet another vital ingredient of the Industrial Revolution.

A small iron industry had existed for centuries in Great Britain, but the development of industry in the second half of the 18th century greatly increased the demand for this iron.

The Birthplace of the Iron Industry

The Darby family made Coalbrookdale the major center of iron production. Visitors from all over Europe came to see and perhaps copy the new methods.

The most important ironmasters were the Darbys of Coalbrookdale. They were responsible for a remarkable series of innovations in the manufacture and use of iron. In 1709, Abraham Darby I (1678–1717) succeeded in smelting good quality iron using coal instead of charcoal. This was an important development, since supplies of charcoal were declining. Abraham Darby III (1750–1789) built the Iron Bridge over the Severn River

—the world's first iron bridge. The methods developed at Coalbrookdale were adapted and improved in other parts of the country, such as Scotland and South Wales, where there were plentiful supplies of coal.

At Blaenavon in South Wales, a large ironworks was built between 1788 and 1789 that employed 350 people. Breaking the ironstone was women's work. A. J. Munby, writing about the ironworks at Blaenavon in the 19th century, observed that:

The iron bridge still stands near Coalbrookdale as a monument to the Darbys' contribution to the Industrial Revolution.

... the girls ... use heavy hammers ... lifting the hammer over their heads and bringing it down with manly skill and force. Fine strong girls they were ... they break stones thus from 6.00 A.M. to 6.00 P.M. every day.

Railway expansion, in particular, depended on the availability of vast quantities of cheap iron. In 1839–1840, Coalbrookdale also supplied wrought-iron plates for the first large iron steamship to use a screw propeller, the *SS Great Britain*.

Wrought Iron

A great advance was made by Henry Cort (1740–1800) in 1784. Cort worked near Portsmouth and supplied the Royal Navy with iron anchors and guns. In the production of wrought iron, he invented the puddling process to remove carbon from the iron. He also developed the rolling mill, which produced bars or plates of wrought iron. These two processes allowed the mass production of cheap wrought iron.

Stronger Than Iron

Thanks to Bessemer, right up to the 1890s Britain was the world's largest steel producer. By 1902, however, it had been overtaken by the United States and Germany.

Further progress came later with the invention of a process that converted iron into steel. Steel, made from iron with a small amount of carbon, is even better and stronger than iron. It is as hard as cast iron, but as flexible as wrought iron. Henry Bessemer (1812–1898) used some Blaenavon pig iron when he developed his process for making steel in 1856. At first, steel was quite expensive and limited to certain fine products—Sheffield steel and cutlery became world famous. But later, using the Bessemer process, the cheap production of large quantities of steel was possible.

Britain's Advantages

In some ways, the Industrial Revolution could be described as the "Slow Revolution." Improvements in many industries, including iron and steel, all took the best part of one hundred years before they could be said to be established and of importance. Yet these industries did develop and, with each stage of development, stimulated further change and growth. The process was continual and persistent. If a key component for industrial progress had been missing, then the story would have been different.

Britain's Industrial Revolution was made possible by the availability of key natural resources, in particular coal and iron. Although there was no great technological revolution in coal-mining, there was a massive increase in coal production. The ready availability of coal and iron made feasible the development of steam engines. Those engines would have been no more than expensive novelties had there not been the iron to build them and cheap coal to drive them.

The profitability of the coal and iron industries encouraged entrepreneurs to invest capital to overcome problems as these industries grew. This capital facilitated the work of men such as Watt and Davy, releasing talent to invent and innovate.

By 1900, "King Coal" employed over one million men to produce more than 200 million tons of coal. About a quarter of the coal was exported.

A German ironworks in 1875. Germany copied many British industrial methods and by 1900 had become a serious commercial rival.

Natural curiosity was one motive for this investment and pace of technological development, but by far the most important incentive was the opportunity to make a fortune. Investors in industry, inventors, and entrepreneurs were discovering, and exploiting, opportunities to become rich or simply richer. However, historians simply do not understand why all inventions occurred when they did. New technology was not always a response to economic pressure. For example, the flying shuttle was invented before the spinning jenny, even though the greater need was for more thread.

The Importance of Inventors

Inventors were talented individuals who often carried out their work on their own or with a single assistant or collaborator (there were no research laboratories). Inventors patented their inventions, that is, they registered their idea with a government agency in order to protect their rights. Yet many ideas were stolen and legal arguments between inventors claiming the rights to a particular idea were rife. At stake could be a great deal of money. Of course, it was impossible to prevent the copying of British techniques on an international level.

The work of individual inventors and improvers was, however, acknowledged at the time. For example, in recognition of his importance, a statue of James Watt was placed in Westminster Abbey in 1819. These words, inscribed on the statue, express the popular sentiment of the industrializing generation:

He enlarged the resources of his country, increased the power of man, and rose to an eminent place among the most illustrious followers of science and real benefactors of the world.

James Watt in his Glasgow workshop. The unit of electric power, the "watt," was named after him.

A REVOLUTION IN TRANSPORTATION

The Need for Better Transportation

One important obstacle to progress in many places was poor systems of transportation. Economic progress was hindered, or even totally obstructed, when people, food, raw materials, and manufactured goods could not be moved around easily. A revolution in industry also required a revolution in transportation.

In the early 18th century, it was difficult and expensive for anyone or anything to travel any distance. Wherever possible, goods were transported on rivers or around the coast by sea. Roads, mostly earth tracks, were usually in a terrible condition. In summer, roads were dusty with hard ruts that could easily break a wheel or a leg. In winter, many of them became hopelessly impassable with mud and potholes. Moreover, goods traveling by road were loaded onto packhorses—anything fragile, such as china and glass, was likely to be broken. For travelers, journeys were long, uncomfortable, and, if they risked travel by coach, very expensive. Arthur Young, writing in 1770, described the difficulties of road transportation:

 I met ruts that I actually measured as four feet deep and floating in mud. The only mending it receives is the tumbling in of some loose stones which jolt a carriage in the most intolerable manner.

Roads and Roadbuilders

The first transportation problem to be tackled was the poor state of the roads. Entrepreneurs, seeing the opportunity to make a profit, set up turnpike trusts, which took over sections of well-used roads and instituted programs of repair and improvement. Travelers had to pay a toll to use these improved roads. Different rates were charged for individual travelers, stagecoaches, wagons, and livestock. Between 1750 and 1791, 1,600 turnpike trusts were set up, and commentators spoke of "turnpike fever" as entrepreneurs eagerly tried to stake out their share of

A stagecoach at a turnpike gate. Even with improvements, road journeys were long, uncomfortable, and, by coach, very expensive.

Thomas Telford was called the "colossus of roads." His Menai Bridge in North Wales is still in use.

this apparently profitable enterprise. Not all turnpikes made a large profit, however, and some trusts tried to maximize profits by skimping on road repairs and thus defeating the purpose of tolls.

A number of civil engineers who were employed by the turnpike trusts developed new methods of building and maintaining roads. Thomas Telford (1757–1834) overcame enormous obstacles to construct a network of roads in the Scottish Highlands. John Macadam (1756–1836) developed a new type of road surface—his "macadamized roads" were sprayed with tar to give a waterproof "tarmac" surface.

As a result of these road improvements, travel speeds improved. Between 1790 and 1830, coaches carrying passengers, mail, and newspapers sped along the turnpikes linking every part of Britain. The journey of 276 miles (444 km) from London to Newcastle, which took six days before the development of turnpikes, took just over one day in 1830. Likewise, the journey of 416 miles (670 km) from London to Edinburgh was reduced from ten days to just two. Despite this, coach travel remained expensive and far beyond the reach of most people.

Canal Mania

For about 50 years between 1780 and 1830, canals provided the solution to some of industry's transportation problems. They were a natural extension to the use of rivers. In France and the Netherlands, canal transportation had already proven successful. In 1757, James Brindley (1716–1772) was employed to build a canal from the Duke of Bridgewater's coal mines at Worsley in Lancashire to nearby Manchester, 10 miles (16 km) away. The Bridgewater Canal was a huge success. While the building costs were about $290,000 (£200,000), around $116,000 (£80,000) was collected each year in tolls. It was not long before the canal was making a hefty profit. Moreover, the canal had the effect of reducing the price of coal in Manchester by about a half. Brindley overcame significant engineering problems to build the Bridgewater Canal, using an aqueduct to cross a river and a tunnel to channel the canal through a hillside.

This portrait made for the Duke of Bridgewater shows him standing by the canal and aqueduct that he paid James Brindley to build.

Brindley's achievement led to the construction of a network of canals. Entrepreneurs formed companies to construct canals wherever it seemed profitable. Brindley's grand plan linked the Thames, Severn, Mersey, and Trent rivers and crossed at Birmingham. Its implementation meant that it became possible to ship goods by river and canal from Birmingham to London, Liverpool, Bristol, or Hull. During the 1790s, so many canals were built that the building phenomenon became known as "canal mania." However, not all the canals were needed and in some cases, there wasn't enough traffic to support the canal. Bankruptcy and loss followed.

The Navvies

The men who built the canals were known as navvies, from the word "navigator." It was hard, heavy work, compounded by poor living conditions in overcrowded huts or tents. Navvies were often subject to exploitation, being overcharged for food and drink by local tradesmen. Before long, they had a reputation for drunkenness and violent behavior. Such behavior, or the fear of it, frightened local people as the canals were being built. This report from Wragby in Lincolnshire is typical:

A dispute arose between the navvies and a baker; the riot began at The Plough—they drove the landlord away, took out the barrels, and drank the beer.... They pelted the baker with his bread; then they attacked the Bottle and Glass and drank the ale.

Canal Decline

Canals were a good means of transporting large quantities of heavy goods, such as coal and building materials. They were also ideal for moving fragile goods and were a major factor in the prosperity of the pottery industry. However, canals were slow (about the speed of a horse) and unsuitable for transporting perishable goods, such as food. Although more comfortable than road travel, they were really too slow as a means of passenger transportation. By the 1830s, the canal system had begun to decline as canals faced the challenge of a far better method of transportation: the railroad.

The entrance to the Regent's Canal at Limehouse, London. The canal carried grain into the city and carried imports from abroad inland.

The Railway Age

The first railways in the late 18th century were no more than horse-drawn wagons carrying coal a short distance along wooden planks and, later, iron rails. These "railroads" were confined almost entirely to coal mines. In the United States, one of these short railways was first used in Boston in 1795 to haul bricks. In 1803, the world's first public goods railway line, from Croydon in Surrey to the Thames River at Wandsworth, was built by William Jessop (1745–1814), a canal engineer. Anyone could pay for his goods to be carried in a horse-drawn truck.

George Stephenson (1781–1848), rightly called the "father of the railways," was not, however, their inventor. Convinced of the advantages of steam locomotion, he improved on the work of others. When he built the Stockton to Darlington line in 1825, he was determined to use steam. The very first train, made up of twelve loaded wagons, a coach, and 21 passenger cars, was hauled by Stephenson's *Locomotion* steam locomotive. It heralded the start of the Railway Age. Stephenson's success led to the construction of the Liverpool to Manchester line in 1830. Working with his son Robert (1803–1859), he managed to build the line across boggy land. Their locomotive, *The Rocket*, reached speeds of over 30 miles per hour (48 kph). This was a significant speed at a time when no one had ever traveled faster than the speed of a horse. At first, some people thought that these speeds would cause brain damage! But the Stephensons' achievements guaranteed that from then on, people and goods were going to travel faster than horses could ever carry them.

Robert Stephenson's *Rocket*. The opening of the Liverpool to Manchester line was marred when William Huskisson, an MP who supported the railway, was knocked down and killed by the *Rocket*.

These pictures show raw materials (top) and livestock (bottom) being transported on the Liverpool to Manchester Railway (1830).

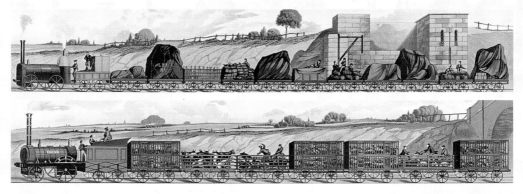

The railways brought many advantages. The cost of transporting raw materials to the factories, and then the finished goods to the shops and markets in the towns, was reduced. These reduced costs were often passed on to customers. Fresh food, such as fish from coastal ports or milk from farms in Somerset or Devon, could be moved quickly and cheaply to urban customers far away. Letters and parcels, too, could be sent quickly to any part of the country.

The People's Trains

Most importantly, the railways allowed people to travel about the country easily and cheaply. For the first time, people could look for jobs more widely, and even commute. There were new opportunities for leisure activities, as well. In 1841, Thomas Cook (1808–1892), a Christian opposed to alcohol, organized the first excursion train to take people from Leicester to nearby Loughborough for a temperance meeting. People so enjoyed the trip that Cook organized other outings and by the 1860s he had become a major travel agent, planning and selling trips by sea and rail all over the world.

Train travel also contributed to the development of the beach resort. Seaside towns such as Brighton, Blackpool, and Southend grew rapidly to accommodate the thousands of people who flocked from the cities on special workmen's excursion trains every summer weekend. Until the advent of the railways, few working people in the towns would ever have been to the seaside or enjoyed walking in the countryside.

The Railway Station (1862) by William Frith. By the 1860s, trains were carrying more than 100 million passengers a year in Britain.

The Railway Industry

The railways were a huge industry in themselves, consuming vast quantities of iron for rails and locomotives, enormous amounts of bricks for tunnels and stations, and many tons of coal to drive the locomotives. In addition, thousands of jobs were created by the railways—often providing employment for those who had lost their jobs when canal- and road-building projects became less popular. Railway towns, with engine sheds and workshops, sprang up in places such as Swindon, Rugby, and Crewe. The population of Crewe zoomed from 203 in 1841 to almost 18,000 thirty years later. At the peak of railway construction, more than 200,000 navvies were at work.

Navvies blasting rocks at Linslade in 1837. With pick-axes, shovels, wheelbarrows, and gunpowder, navvies built almost 20,000 miles (32,000 km) of railway between 1825 and 1880.

Exporting the Railways

Before long, other countries followed Britain's lead. In 1841, British navvies were employed to construct the French line from Paris to Rouen. It was the beginning of one of Britain's greatest exports. British engineers built railroads all over the world (for example, Prussia, Italy, Austria-Hungary, India, South America, Canada, and Australia) and British workshops supplied many of the steam locomotives that were run on them. The growth of railways abroad was actually a case of Britain exporting the means of her eventual undoing. The export of railways directly aided industrial development in Britain's European neighbors, creating serious industrial competition with Britain.

In the United States, a British-made steam engine, the *Stourbridge Lion*, caused great excitement when it made the 16.1-mile (26-km) trip from Honesdale to Carbondale in Pennsylvania at 10 miles per hour (16 kph). According to one spectator, it resembled a mammoth grasshopper. Before long, the Americans were building their own locomotives and an extensive rail network. In 1869, the "transcontinental railroad," 1,775 miles (2,856 km) long, linked Chicago and San Francisco.

In January 1831, the *Best Friend* locomotive started America's first regular passenger service from Charleston, South Carolina. Six months later it blew up, killing the fireman.

The Gauge Mistake

Americans, like most others, learned from British mistakes. George Stephenson had based the width between the rails, known as the gauge, on the width of horse-drawn wagons. This gauge of four feet, eight-and-a-half inches (143.5 cm) is still the standard width of British railways. It is really too narrow—wider trains are more stable and can carry far more people and goods. Isambard Brunel (1806–1859), another great railway engineer, failed to persuade the government to adopt his gauge of seven feet, two inches (220 cm). The matter was settled by a Royal Commission that decided upon the narrower gauge, because 90 percent of railways already built used the four feet, eight-and-a-half-inch gauge. The Gauge Act of 1846 made the standard gauge compulsory for all future railways and is still in force today. But most other countries, having seen Britain's railways, chose a wider gauge for their own.

Besides being a brilliant railway engineer, Isambard Brunel, known as the "Little Giant," built Clifton Suspension Bridge, Paddington Station, and the first ocean liners such as the *SS Great Britain*.

A Runaway Success

An improved transportation system was an essential prerequisite for economic expansion. It was not a coincidence that improvements in transportation accompanied developments in industry and agriculture. The growth of trade was both the stimulus and the beneficiary of better roads, canals, and railroads. Although there was no turnpike system since each turnpike road was the result of local initiatives, nevertheless most turnpikes were the result of growing traffic on those routes. Far from being haphazard, most major turnpikes became part of a network that served the areas where trade and industry were growing.

But far more significant for industry were the canals. The problem had always been in transporting bulky goods, especially coal. Steam engines, and all kinds of industrial processes, needed coal. The first canals were built specifically for the movement of coal. Even many agricultural products were heavy and bulky, such as potatoes and turnips. The canals provided a cheap way of transporting these goods just as industrial development and growing towns needed them. Both roads and canals were important in developing skills for the civil engineers and navvies who actually built them. This experience and knowledge helps to explain why the transportation revolution, with the construction of the bulk of the railway network, took place in only twenty years, 1830–1850.

This map of the Bridgewater Canal appeared in a magazine in 1766. People marveled at this engineering achievement.

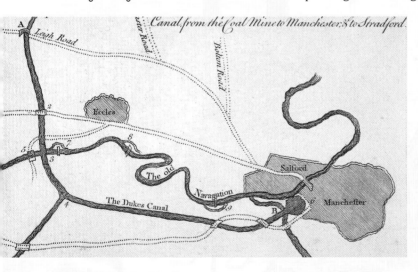

The Railway Revolution

The early momentum of the Industrial Revolution would have come to a halt had it not been for the arrival of the railways. By the 1830s, there were signs that economic growth was beginning to slow down. The railways helped the Industrial Revolution move into a second and even more profitable phase that lasted until at least 1900. Probably no other single development had such a tremendous impact on people's lives. By 1855, the major

London's first railway station was Euston, opened in 1837. It was followed by King's Cross, Paddington, Victoria, and St. Pancras.

Engineering feats such as the Kilsby Tunnel, Wales, 1839, thrilled and amazed Victorians. However, they were achieved at a considerable price in terms of human accidents and injuries.

part of the British railway network, about 8,000 miles (13,000 km), was complete.

Some people, fearful of its effects, tried to hold back the growth of the railways. Farmers feared competition from food that would be brought into towns from far-off areas. Other farmers were worried that the trains would upset their animals. Some towns would not permit the railways and Oxford University would not allow one any nearer than Didcot, about 10 miles (16 km) away.

The Duke of Wellington was concerned that working men might move around and cause trouble! This fear was expressed by Colonel Sibthorpe, Member of Parliament for Lincoln, speaking in 1844:

Next to civil war, railways are the greatest curse to the country.

But no amount of opposition could stop the railways. They were simply too important and too great an opportunity to make large profits. The Victorians were in awe of the achievement in building the lines with their tunnels, bridges, and imposing stations. The speed of the trains impressed everyone, and entrepreneurs were excited by the prospect of increased sales.

The railways ensured continued economic growth. Not only did they provide employment but they boosted those industries that supplied them with the equipment and materials they needed. By spurring the growth of the coal, iron, and manufacturing industries, the railways helped move the economy away from its previous dependence on the textile industry. To people in the 1830s, the railways were a revolutionary new form of transportation. To historians, they are both a symbol of the Industrial Revolution and a cause of later prosperity.

CHAPTER FOUR

WORKING IN THE FACTORIES

Was the Working Class Better Off?

The northern industrial town of Bolton, 1848. Was life really better for those who lived in the new factory towns than it had been for previous generations?

One result of the factory system was the development of a new social group—the industrial working class. These people lived in the towns and worked in the factories. There is no agreement among historians as to whether the working class was actually better off because of industrialization after 1750. There is no doubt that wealth increased and Britain became a prosperous country during the 1800s, but does this mean that everyone's standard of living rose as a result of the Industrial Revolution?

Factory wages were higher than those in agriculture, and many urban workers had a higher standard of living than did workers in rural areas. As the costs of food and manufactured goods went down, people could afford to buy more. But at the same time, the factory system created an entirely new way of life and work. James Kay-Shuttleworth (1804–1877) wrote in 1832:

Whilst the engine runs, the people must work—men, women, and children are yoked together with iron and steam. The animal machine is chained fast to the iron machine, which knows no suffering and weariness.

Studies of the conditions of people living and working in factory towns undoubtedly show that they were harsh and painful. But for centuries, the way of life in the countryside had also been tough and often quite wretched. Agriculture was vulnerable to many adversities. It was mainly seasonal and did not provide continuous employment throughout the year. A poor harvest spelled disaster for landless laborers (and there were many of those). Loss of livestock through disease was a catastrophe, and at times of particular hardship, some people starved to death. It is therefore difficult to assess to what extent life was better or worse than it had been before the Industrial Revolution.

Laissez-Faire

Life was certainly different. For the majority of people, the main effect of the Industrial Revolution was that they were the first generations of their families to work in factories and to live in towns. Too often, changes in working and production methods were implemented with little concern for those most affected by them. Long hours characterized working lives. Early factories were noisy, unhealthy, and often dangerous places. The government stuck to a policy known as *laissez-faire*, which meant, quite literally, to leave things alone. This meant that the government was unwilling to interfere in the running of industry. Lord Liverpool, the prime minister, speaking in 1812, supported this approach:

Lord Liverpool, the longest-serving prime minister in the 1800s, had a reputation for dealing with working-class protest with cruel firmness.

It is undoubtedly true that the less commerce and manufacture are meddled with, the more likely they are to prosper.

Laissez-faire was a strongly held approach to government. For many years, it effectively blocked attempts to pass new laws that would have protected people at work. The factory system increased the overall wealth of the nation and, in the long term, brought benefits to everybody. But for those who had grown up in rural areas and migrated to the towns seeking employment, working in those first factories must have been difficult to get used to. One visitor's description of a factory in 1840 portrays the typical working environment:

The wracking noise of engines, the hell of sounds. The dragging, wearing monotony of the machine; the stifling heat; the unbroken noise; the necessity of constant action on the part of the workers; render the place and the employment all but intolerable.

Workers in this 19th-century cloth-dying factory had no health and safety laws to protect them or a trade union to speak for them.

Factory Conditions

In the United States, as late as 1900, children made up one-fourth of the workforce working thirteen hours a day.

Children as young as 3 or 4, as well as adults, were employed in factories. There was no compulsory schooling until 1880, and poverty forced many parents to send their children to work in the factories. The advantage for the factory owner was that children were cheaper to employ than adults. One result of child labor was that it kept down the wages paid to adults. In 1833, the cotton mills employed 84,000 children on wages that were roughly one-fifth of the adult male wage. In the factories, the children collected waste from under the machines and joined broken threads together. Their small size meant they could crawl under, or even inside, machines without having to turn them off. Such work could be dangerous and led to some horrible injuries and deaths. Evidence given to Parliament in 1841 tells of,

These factory children in Yorkshire in 1814 look quite happy. How reliable is this source, when we compare it with other evidence?

A girl at Stockport … carried by her clothing round an upright shaft; her thighs were broken, her ankles dislocated. A boy's shirt caught in a machine; his arm was torn off and his head injured.

Working hours for all workers were long, with very few breaks. One witness told Members of Parliament in 1831 that sometimes, during the busy season, children as young as 8 worked from 3 A.M. until 10.30 P.M. This was exceptional, but the normal working day was at least twelve hours.

Abuse and corporal punishment were used by the overseers to force the children to work harder. Overseers were usually paid on the basis of how much was produced by the workers in their charge.

Conditions in the Mines

However, working conditions in the mines were probably far worse. Miners were often better paid than factory workers, but conditions were poor. Many women and children worked as putters, hauling coal along the tunnels. They often worked in darkness and had to drag heavy carts on all fours along very low passages. In Scotland, women carted coal in wicker baskets on their backs up a long series of ladders that eventually reached the surface. Sometimes, the basket would break and spill the coal onto the unfortunate person lower down on the ladder. An extract from a report to Parliament in 1842 describes working conditions for a teenage girl who labored in a mine:

Agnes Kerr, 15, was 9 years old when she commenced carrying coal; makes 18–20 journeys a day; a journey is about 400 meters [1,312 feet]; has to ascend many ladders; can carry about 75 kilos [165 pounds].

Children being winched down a mine shaft in 1842. Gradually, stronger wire rope replaced hemp rope, making the operation slightly less dangerous.

Lord Shaftesbury, a reformer, visiting the coal mines of the Black Country, 1840–1842. There he witnessed, at first hand, the conditions in which children worked.

The Reformers

From all this, we can see that, for some people at least, the human cost of economic progress was harsh. What is difficult for people nearly two hundred years later to understand is why it took so long for anyone to improve the situation. There were people who were horrified by these conditions and who were determined to change them, but these reformers faced strong resistance from those who argued, in the spirit of *laissez-faire*, that the government had no right to interfere in the running of private companies. Factory owners warned that shorter hours and better conditions would drive their companies into bankruptcy and cause even more misery by creating mass unemployment. For their part, the government held to the policy of *laissez-faire*.

Robert Owen

Many of the reformers were factory owners themselves, although they were not usually popular with other factory owners. The best known was Robert Owen (1771–1858), who proved that it was possible to run a successful factory and, at the same time, treat the workers well. Owen was one of the first to draw attention to the evils of the factory system. Throughout his life, he sided with working-class people and was a strong supporter of trade unions.

At New Lanark in Scotland, Robert Owen practiced his enlightened ideas as a factory owner.

A dancing class at Owen's school at New Lanark. Establishing the school fulfilled Owen's greatest ambition.

Owen operated his father-in-law's textile factory at New Lanark in Scotland. He was convinced that it was wrong to employ young children in factories and he was an outspoken critic of the working conditions in the majority of factories. Most other factory owners claimed that if they reduced working hours, raised wages, and ceased to employ children, their businesses would be ruined. They also said that factory work was good for the children!

At New Lanark, Owen reduced working hours to ten-and-a-half hours per day. Wages were increased and were even paid when workers were too sick to work, a practice unheard of in the early 19th century. Owen also set about improving the housing of his workers. He refused to employ any child under the age of 10. He aspired to increasing the age limit to 12, but that seemed impossible. Instead of working in factories, Owen believed that children should go to school—he set up the first actual nursery school in Britain. Other factory owners criticized Owen for being "soft" and were enraged when their own workers began to demand that they should be treated in the same way. Owen was warned that his business would collapse, but instead, New Lanark prospered.

New Laws

Working with other reformers, Owen created the Ten Hour Movement to campaign for a ten-hour working day. In Parliament the reformers were successful in instituting inquiries into children's working conditions. The evidence they unearthed shocked many Members of Parliament. Against strong opposition from factory owners, laws were eventually passed that provided some protection for women and children in the textile industry.

A government inspector visits a factory where children are employed. Factory Acts and inspectors marked the end of *laissez-faire*.

The 1833 Factory Act ruled that no children under the age of 9 were to be employed and those aged 9 to 13 were not allowed to work more than nine hours a day. Children aged 13 to 18 were not allowed to work for more than twelve hours a day and were not permitted to work at night. To enforce the law, four factory inspectors were appointed. One initial problem in implementing this law was that it was not always possible to prove how old children were. Frequently, children lied about their ages because, however unpleasant the job was, their families depended on the income. The official recording of births started with the Registration Act (1836), and after a few years it was possible to check on a child's age.

The 1844 Factory Act ruled that children between the ages of 8 and 13 could work up to six-and-a-half hours a day and had to receive three hours of schooling on five days of the week. The Act said that young people and women must work for no more than twelve hours a day and for the first time declared that dangerous machinery had to be fenced in. The Ten Hours Act of 1847 ruled that women and young persons must not work for more than ten hours a day. While these laws appear fairly limited, particularly as they only applied to the textile industry, they were passed against very strong opposition from the factory owners and were huge victories for the reformers.

Lord Shaftesbury worked tirelessly to improve conditions, but he was still opposed to allowing working-class men to vote.

Reform Presses On

Another reformer, Lord Shaftesbury (1801–1885), succeeded in persuading Parliament in 1842 to ban the employment of boys under the age of 10 and the employment of women underground in mines. Mine owners, many of whom were members of the House of Lords, fought hard against this law. Shaftesbury was appalled by their attitude. Speaking of the mine owners in 1842 he said:

Never have I seen such a display of selfishness, unfeeling to every human sentiment.

Opponents of reform continued to argue that such laws would destroy the profitability of British industry and render it incapable of competing with foreign companies. In spite of all their fears, factory owners did not seem to suffer as a result of these reforms and their profits continued to rise. Unfortunately, the workers, whom the reforms were supposed to help, often did suffer. The women and children who were disqualified from working by the new laws often underwent hardship. Some women were still employed at coal mines sorting coal on the surface, but employers were forced to employ more men. This benefited some families but, overall, especially in the mines, led to a reduction in the number of people employed. Without any kind of financial help from the state, unemployment caused grave hardship.

Although they could no longer work underground, many women, such as this worker in the 1890s, had surface jobs at the mines.

Slow Reform

Nineteenth-century observers of industrial change held widely conflicting views. Their disagreements help explain why it was even difficult to protect children. Richard Oastler, a Yorkshire land agent, was angry about the treatment of factory children when he wrote to his local newspaper in 1830:

Thousands of little children both male and female, from seven to fourteen years, are daily compelled to labor from six o'clock in the morning to seven in the evening with only—Britons, blush whilst you read it!—with only thirty minutes allowed for eating and recreation.

However, Dr. Ure, a medical practitioner, writing in 1835, thought that the employment of young children in factories was perfectly acceptable:

They (children) seemed to be always cheerful and alert, taking pleasure in the light play of their muscles....The work of these lively elves seemed to resemble a sport.

Although arguments over the employment of children have ended, some debates by modern historians mirror the arguments of the 19th century. Contemporaries and modern-day historians have argued that, in spite of poor working conditions, most factory workers benefited from falling prices and regular employment. These historians, known as "optimists," are challenged by "pessimists" who argue that any apparent improvement in the standard of living was offset by the long working hours in poor and often dangerous conditions.

At first, the scope of the 19th-century law was very limited in the protection it gave to industrial workers. Gradually, the supporters of *laissez-faire* were forced to retreat and it was reluctantly accepted that the law should give some protection to women and children.

Pictures like this shocked the public and helped to persuade Parliament to pass the Mines Act of 1842.

Members of the House of Lords usually put up powerful resistance to reform and progress was slow. Working-class opinions were ignored.

No action was taken to protect men, because the relationship between a working man and his employer was regarded as an entirely voluntary and private arrangement. A worker, it was believed, could decide for himself whether or not to take a particular job with the wages and conditions that went with it. A factory owner should be able to run his business as he saw fit, free from government interference. Of course, it was not that simple. Men had to work and, in many places, there was no choice as to whom they worked for. If they did not take a job at the local mine, ironworks, or factory, then they and their family could either starve or suffer the indignity and harshness of the workhouse. Many wealthy people took the convenient view that this social order had been ordained by God and should not be interfered with.

Reforming Roles

Reformers used different ways to promote improvement. Elizabeth Gaskell (1810–1865) used her position as a writer to describe the dreadful conditions of factory workers in Manchester. She shocked some of her middle-class readers when she expressed the anger felt by many working-class people. In her novel *Mary Barton* (1848), one of her characters exclaims:

Don't think to come over me with the old tale, that the rich know nothing of the trials of the poor. I say, if they don't know, they ought to know. We are their slaves as long as we can work; we pile up their fortunes with the sweat of our brows; and yet we are to live as separate as if we were in two worlds.

Besides writing about poor working conditions, Elizabeth Gaskell took food to local unemployed mill-workers who could not feed their families.

Today, in countries where industrialization has been slow, child labor, and long working hours with little protection for workers endure just as they did in 19th-century Britain. Just as *laissez-faire* held back government intervention that could have softened the ill-effects of industrialization in the 19th century, so present-day inaction allows the exploitation of workers to continue. The middle classes in the 19th century enjoyed cheaper coal and food with little thought to those who produced it, in the same way that the prosperous West gives little thought to those who produce the cheap imported food and clothing that it consumes.

47

THE NEW INDUSTRIAL TOWNS

Urban Growth

Change creates a momentum of its own, creating ever more change. During the 19th century, towns grew at a phenomenal rate. Large urban settlements developed around the sites of new factories, their growth brought about by inadequate transportation and long working hours, which meant that workers were obliged to live in close proximity to their places of work. Industrial towns grew rapidly and haphazardly with almost no planning and no provision of public services. Parks and green spaces were virtually nonexistent and air quality was poor, polluted by smoke from thousands of chimneys. The Industrial Revolution gave rise to large, dismal industrial cities that were overcrowded, dirty, unhealthy, and the breeding ground of a range of problems for future generations.

Growth of Towns, 1801–51, from Official Census Figures

	1801	*1851*
London	1,100,000	2,600,000
Glasgow	77,000	345,000
Manchester	75,000	338,000
Birmingham	71,000	265,000

Glasgow grew very quickly during the Industrial Revolution, but the streets were unpaved and there was no proper water supply or garbage collection.

Homes for the Workers

Frederick Engels, co-author with Karl Marx of *The Communist Manifesto*, demanded that power should be in the hands of the working class.

For the middle class, there was a plentiful supply of comfortable homes, usually on paved streets with proper drainage and a supply of clean water. But industrial wages only stretched to low rents on poor properties. Working-class homes were built as quickly and cheaply as possible. Since building was largely unregulated, builders crammed as many houses as they could into the smallest possible area of land. Many homes were built back-to-back with no yard and very little light. Each house had one or two rooms upstairs and the same number downstairs.

Factory towns grew in the shape of countless long rows of these houses strung along narrow streets or alleyways. Because builders used cheap materials, the bricks were often porous and the walls were constantly damp. Frederick Engels (1820–1895), a German socialist writer whose father owned a cotton factory in Manchester, wrote in 1845:

Back-to-back housing was typical in all factory towns. There were no gardens and little light or fresh air.

All conceivable evils are heaped upon the heads of the poor ... they are penned in dozens of single rooms, so that the air which they breathe at night is enough in itself to stifle them. They are given damp dwellings, cellar dens that are not waterproof from below ... Even in Manchester the people are pale, lank, narrow-chested, hollow-eyed ghosts incapable of the slightest energetic expression.

Overcrowding

Overcrowding was a major problem. A family of perhaps five or six people would often live in a single room. A typical case of 1842 is that of a father, mother, and twelve children in the Midlands sleeping in a room about 12 feet (3 1/2 m) square with one small window. The ceiling was so low that it was possible for a man to stand up fully only in the center of the room. Worst off of all were the cellar dwellers. It has been estimated that about 18,000 people lived in cellars in Manchester and Liverpool in 1845. The cellars were even darker and damper than the rest of the house. Some people, because they were poor, kept a pig with them in the cellar, which they could either sell or use for food.

Water and Sewage

Water supply and sanitation in working-class areas was poor and often very inconvenient. The responsibility to ensure that a proper water supply was provided to new houses belonged to no one. People used communal privies that emptied into cesspits. Sometimes, families kept their excrement outside their door for a dung collector who then sold it to farmers as manure. They had to collect their water for drinking and washing from public pumps that were often unreliable and produced dirty water. The roads were unpaved, undrained, and frequently muddy with all kinds of waste.

In 1840, Dr Southwood-Smith, a fierce critic of these unhealthy living conditions, described what he saw in the Bethnal Green and Whitechapel districts of London:

Even in the late 1800s, many houses had no water supply. People often had to carry their water from a long distance, such as these residents of Bethnal Green in the East End of London, 1863.

Uncovered sewers, stagnant ditches and ponds, gutters always full of putrefying [rotting] matter, nightmen's yards, and privies, the soil of which lies openly exposed, and is seldom or never removed. It is not possible for any language to convey an adequate conception of the poisonous condition in which large portions of both these districts always remain, winter and summer, in dry and in rainy seasons, from the masses of putrefying matter which are allowed to accumulate.

Water for drinking or washing was often contaminated. Water was often sold and the better-off assumed that by paying for water it would be cleaner. A great deal of the domestic water supply came from rivers and streams that were also used for dumping sewage. Open sewers, such as the Fleet Ditch, flowed through London into the Thames. In spite of it being heavily polluted, many people relied on water taken from the Thames. Often people would resort to water from stagnant and dirty ditches for cooking and washing.

Disease and Death

An inevitable consequence of such poor living conditions was disease and illness. Child mortality was high throughout the period of the Industrial Revolution —162 per 1,000 in 1850. In Liverpool in 1842, more than 60 percent of children died before they reached

ICOSM dedicated to the London Water Companies. THESE ALL MONSTERS! ALL PRODIGIOUS THINGS. HYDRAS AND GORGONS AND CHIMERAS DIRE.

TER SOUP commonly called **THAMES WATER**, being a correct representation of that precious stuff doled out to us.

This cartoon by George Cruikshank highlighted the appalling pollution of the Thames River, from which Londoners got their water supply.

the age of 5. New epidemics of serious diseases spread rapidly in the overcrowded cities and towns.

The most feared disease was cholera. Together with typhoid fever and dysentry, cholera was spread when people drank water or ate food that had been contaminated by the excrement of people suffering from these illnesses. In 1831, 1,500 people in Liverpool were killed by cholera, but in 1849 over 5,000 people in Liverpool died of the disease. At the same time, 15,000 people died from the disease in London. The spread of any disease was made worse by the malnutrition and poor diet of many people. However, no one was safe from these diseases. Prince Albert, Queen Victoria's husband, died in 1861 from typhoid fever, which was blamed on poor toilet facilities at Windsor Castle.

Combating Disease

Lack of medical knowledge also made it hard to combat disease. A widely held belief, even as late as the 1840s, was that diseases such as cholera were spread by "miasma"—bad smells in the air. During one cholera outbreak in London, cannons were fired to disturb the air and supposedly disperse the smells!

Average Age of Death in 1842 in Town and Rural Areas

	Manchester (factory town)	*Rutland* (rural)
Professional persons	38	52
Farmers and tradesmen	20	41
Mechanics and laborers	17	38

Rapidly growing towns with a high death rate created another problem. Cemeteries and burial grounds became overcrowded. If burial grounds flooded or if underground streams ran through them, this could further pollute drinking water. Sometimes, people kept dead bodies at home until they could save up to pay for the burial. Delays like this, which could last for days or even weeks, added to the danger of disease.

Benjamin Disraeli, Queen Victoria's favorite prime minister, promoted laws to improve public health and working conditions.

Two Nations

The lifestyles of the different social classes were markedly different. The novelist Benjamin Disraeli (1804–1881), who later became prime minister, thought that the gulf between the rich and the poor was so great that it was as if they lived in separate countries or, in his own words, "two nations." But what Disraeli expressed in words was clear for everyone to see around them in the first half of the 19th century. Questions of poverty and the consequent responsibility of the wealthy were hotly debated.

There were a few well-off men and women who sided with the plight of the poor. Some of them were reformers who sought to improve conditions, while others were Radicals who wanted political changes that would lead to better conditions for working-class people. Yet most well-off people were steadfast in resisting improvements, and were able to remain so because the working class had no political power to bring about change.

Lifestyle Revolution

Urbanization, the growth of towns, was an important feature of the Industrial Revolution. By 1851, there were eighteen million Britons, the majority of whom lived in towns and cities. It was a significant change in the British way of life from that of a nation of rural dwellers to one of townspeople. Some towns grew up alongside the new factories. Other towns grew as industry of all kinds expanded. In 1851, 75 percent of laborers did not work in factories but in ironworks, shipyards, glass works, and thousands of workshops. Yet they shared similar living conditions with those who lived in factory towns. Whereas improvements and developments in industry were pursued promptly, attempts to make life in the towns more bearable were slow.

Picking Up the Bill

Poor living conditions were evident from the beginnings of the first industrial towns. The government did not respond to the revolutionary change going on in the nation. Holding to its policy of interfering as little as possible, it showed no interest in setting standards for the new towns.

After a long day working in the factories, exhausted workers returned to overcrowded and filthy homes.

A typical street scene in Victorian Oldham. The issue for historians is why it took so long to improve conditions.

This left progress to the direction of each individual town, but town authorities lacked the powers that were necessary to bring about effective action. Besides which, there was a conflict of interest. Who would end up paying for improvements? The cost of improvements such as sewage, drainage, and paving would fall to the local taxpayers (the better-off). Yet these people were rarely willing to pay to clean up the living conditions of others, even if those others were their own workers. Better standards of building, which gave more light and space to a house's inhabitants, would hurt the profits of builders and developers. Factory workers could not pay higher rents for better properties as long as child labor and the drive for maximum profits kept wages as low as possible.

Many of those in the towns who held political power therefore had an economic interest in resisting improvements. In addition, there was usually a proper water supply provided to the districts where people could pay for it. Disraeli's two nations remained very much in evidence in almost all industrial towns. The Reverend R. Parkinson said of Manchester in 1842:

There is no town in the world where the distance between the rich and poor is so great, or the barrier between them so difficult to be crossed.

THE TURN OF PROTEST AND SELF-HELP

Protest: The Luddites

Eventually, the changes of the Industrial Revolution were certain to provoke a reaction from those who felt threatened or who suffered from the ill-effects of industrial change. Moreover, at a time when change was little experienced during a person's lifetime and when children supposed that their lives would be much like those of their parents, change was particularly hard for people to cope with.

Hand-loom weavers could not compete with factory mass production.

Factories, with their new machines, gradually destroyed the livelihoods of skilled domestic workers, such as weavers. Thousands of hand-loom weavers saw their wages fall or lost their work altogether. It was impossible for a hand-weaver to compete with a machine. In 1811–1812, groups of skilled hand-workers in the woolen and lace industries started to attack and smash the machines that were ruining them. They called themselves "Luddites," after Ned Ludd, their general. Almost certainly, Ned Ludd never actually existed, but this mythical leader baffled the authorities as they sought to arrest him.

Thousands of machines were smashed with a hammer called "Great Enoch." The violence of the Luddite attacks frightened factory owners and the government. Both feared that the attacks could be the start of a violent revolution against the wealthy, with scenes similar to those witnessed during the French Revolution of 1789. Consequently, the government acted harshly to crush the Luddites. A law of 1812 made machine-breaking punishable by death. Troops moved into areas of Luddite activity, such as Yorkshire, and huge rewards were offered for information that would lead to arrests. Eventually, 70 Luddites were arrested and put on trial at York Castle. Convicted, 17 men were hanged in front of a silent crowd at a public execution.

Following scenes like this one, the machine breakers were ruthlessly pursued and punished.

There was a great deal of public sympathy from ordinary people for the Luddites—it was understood that they were protecting the way they made a living and looked after their families. Although Luddite attacks continued off and on for a few years, the government's tough policy was successful. It was too dangerous to be a Luddite. The judge who sentenced the Luddites to death in 1813 declared:

> *The law of the land will always be too strong for its assailants, and those who defy the law will, in the end, be subdued by the law, and be compelled to submit to its justice or its mercy.*

Fear of Revolution

Following the French Revolution in 1789, the British government became increasingly worried that demands made by working people could lead to revolution. In 1799 and 1800, they passed strict laws that made it illegal for groups of workers to meet together to try to improve their working conditions. These laws, called the Combination Acts because they forbade people combining or joining together, remained in force until 1824. Yet these laws did not hinder people's determination to improve their lives.

The execution of Louis XVI during the French Revolution. Protests in Britain were often mercilessly crushed for fear of a similar revolution.

Joseph Hume (1777–1855), a Radical politician, was largely responsible for the repeal of the Combination Acts.

Robert Owen believed that trade unions were the worker's best means of improvement. His admirers called him "a prophet."

Protest: The Trade Unions

Under the Combination Acts, it was illegal for groups of people to press for better pay or shorter working hours. However, workers were permitted to join together for the purpose of mutual insurance against sickness, old age, or death (there was no official system of insurance). These combinations of workers were known as friendly societies.

A few Members of Parliament, known as Radicals, succeeded in repealing the Combination Laws in 1824. This encouraged attempts to create a national trade union organization. Most unions were small and limited to particular towns or factories. If all workers were members of a single union, it was argued, they would be strong enough to force employers and the government to yield to their demands. Robert Owen, the factory reformer, was an enthusiastic supporter of a single union and promoted the Grand National Consolidated Trades Union (GNCTU) in 1834. He described the purpose of such a union to be for the working classes, to

provide themselves with every species of power; and by a general strike they might bring their superiors to any terms of accommodation.

Owen's proposal was welcomed by most workers, but the forces ranged against Owen and the GNCTU, which included the government and most other factory owners, were powerful and determined. As workers flocked to join the GNCTU, the government became alarmed and decided on strong measures to deal with them.

The Tolpuddle Martyrs

On February 24, 1834, the authorities struck. George Loveless and five fellow members of the Friendly Society of Agricultural Laborers in Tolpuddle, Dorset, were arrested. They were accused, not of belonging to a union, which was perfectly legal, but of making an illegal oath. Fearful that they would be in trouble with the farmers who employed them, Loveless and his companions had made a secret promise to one another not to tell anyone else the names of union members. Making such a promise in secret was actually against the law, although this was little known. More importantly, it provided an opportunity for the government to attack the union.

The Tolpuddle Martyrs, as their supporters called them, were sentenced to seven years' transportation

The largest demonstration London had ever seen—50,000 supporters—protested vainly at the sentencing of the Tolpuddle Martyrs.

(exile in Australia). There was a huge outcry against the sentence and the men were released after serving four years of their sentences. George Loveless, one of the Tolpuddle Martyrs, wrote these words just after he had been sentenced.

God is our guide! No swords we draw,
We kindle not war's battle fires,
By reason, union, justice, law,
We claim the birthright of our sires;
We raise the watchword "Liberty"
We will, we will, we will be free!

Unionism Halted

The aim of the government to destroy trade unionism was largely achieved. Workers became frightened of the possible consequences of joining a union and the GNCTU soon collapsed. It was simply too difficult to organize a single large union, especially when it faced such strong opposition. Some quite large groups of workers in unions refused to join and there were many disagreements within the GNCTU.

After the failure of the GNCTU, many workers looked for other ways to improve their living and working conditions. It was not until 1851 that the first really successful and permanent trade union was established, the Amalgamated Society of Engineers, for skilled workers. Under the Trade Union Act of 1871, unions and their funds were legally recognized and protected. Unskilled workers had to wait until the 1880s when the London match-girls' strike of 1888, followed by the London dockers' strike the following year, demonstrated that effective unions for all workers were possible.

Self-Help: Cooperation

In the 1830s, Robert Owen promoted the ideas of cooperation. Owen was opposed to the capitalist system, or private ownership of business, in which the owners of industry were concerned only with maximizing their profits. His idealism even took him to the United States, where he created a village, New Harmony, in Indiana. It was to be a "village of cooperation" in which all the work would be shared fairly and everyone would have an equal share in what was produced. In reality, there were too many disagreements between the villagers, and Owen's experiment failed. His attempt to set up a worker's cooperative in England in which people swapped their labor for goods, instead of using money, was also a failure.

Yet Owen's cooperative principles inspired others. In 1844, 28 flannel weavers set up a successful cooperative store on Toad Lane, Rochdale. They wanted to provide an alternative to the commercial shopkeeper who often charged high prices for poor-quality goods. By banding together they could sell good-quality basic items, such as flour, tea, and butter, to their members and then split any profits fairly among themselves.

The "Rochdale Principles" by which the cooperative society was governed were: open and voluntary membership, democratic control (one vote per member), fixed and limited interest on share capital, return of surplus to members pro rata to their purchases, sale of pure and unadulterated goods, and provision for education. Ultimately, the ambition of cooperators was to create a society based on cooperation rather than competition between businesses.

The Rochdale cooperative shop was a great success. Co-operative shops began to appear in many industrial northern towns and, by the 1880s, they could be found all over Britain. In addition to running shops, many cooperative societies also organized social activities and trips, and even some educational classes.

Robert Owen planned to build his cooperative village, New Harmony, on this site on the Wabash River. Owen was even invited to address President James Monroe and members of Congress on his plans for New Harmony.

Growth of the Cooperative Movement

Year	Number of societies	Number of members	Total sales (In British Pounds)
1844	1(Rochdale)	28	–
1875	1,266	437,000	$16,090,000 (£3,218,000)
1900	1,439	1,707,000	$250,270,000 (£50,054,000)
1914	1,385	3,504,000	$439,900,000 (£87,980,000)

The Rochdale Pioneers—their cooperative was not the first in Britain, but its principles were adopted by cooperatives nationwide.

Self-Help: Friendly Societies

In addition to the cooperative movement, there was enthusiastic working-class support for a range of other self-help organizations. Friendly societies sprang up to provide some security for people before the state provided any sickness benefit, medical benefit, or unemployment benefit. Members paid small amounts weekly into insurance and savings funds. It was difficult for people on low wages to make any provision for the possibility that they wouldn't have any wages at all. Yet most families experienced times when at least one member was jobless or too ill to go to work and there would be no money coming in.

Before the Welfare State was created in the 1940s, friendly societies filled an important need. Besides providing a practical financial service, the societies also organized social activities and created a sense of security and belonging for their members. The largest society, the Oddfellows, enrolled 434,000 members in 1874.

59

Resisting Working-Class Demands

One thing that clouded the lives of industrialists, the government, and members of the royal family in the early 19th century was fear of working-class protest. They recognized that industrialization was raising many grievances, but self-interest and *laissez-faire* government policies meant those grievances were ignored. Political power was held firmly in the hands of the landed classes. The way Members of Parliament were elected had remained unchanged for hundreds of years and was hopelessly out of date. Before the Reform Act of 1832, industrial towns such as Manchester and Leeds had no Members of Parliament while Old Sarum, where no one lived, had two Members chosen by the local landowner. Consequently, Parliament was quite out of touch with the needs and problems of the industrial areas. This, and the fear of revolution, helps to explain why the authorities were so quick to stamp out any attempts at protest by the working class, who made up the majority of the people.

This cartoon shows Lord John Russell, one of the framers of the 1832 Reform Act, trampling those whose privileges it ended.

A Chartist in the 1830s—all Chartists signed a Charter that demanded universal suffrage, a secret ballot, no property qualifications for MPs (members of Parliament), salaries for MPs, annual elections, and equal electoral districts.

The Legacy of the Luddites

Some historians portray the Luddites as brave men who were seeking to protect their standard of living and dignity in the face of enormous industrial changes. Another interpretation is that the Luddites were no more than a doomed movement, fearful of the future and seeking to prevent industrial progress. Working-class leaders learned that, brave or not, they were not able to triumph over the authorities with their soldiers, prisons, and hangman's noose.

Working-class activity in the 19th century shows a progression from direct action, which was bound to fail, to trade unions and to the Chartists. Chartism was a political campaign that sought to gain the vote for all working men. When this failed, self-help organizations seemed to be the only answer to working-class needs. Because they had the blessing of the government and employers, these organizations were allowed to flourish. In time, as they demonstrated against many people's judgment that working-class people were responsible, they paved the way toward a slow and grudging acceptance of trade unions, the right to vote, and a political party. One hundred years after the Combination Act of 1800, the Labor Party, a political party for working-class people, was born.

The Chartists met in 1848 to demand that every man should have the vote. Political power would have helped achieve other working-class demands.

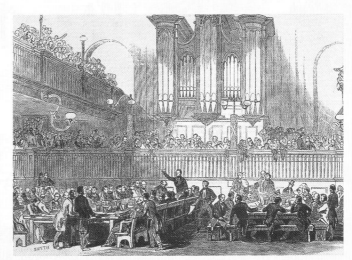

REFORM AND IMPROVEMENT

CHAPTER SEVEN

The Cost of Poverty

The growth of industry and the expansion of towns had been accompanied by disease, overcrowding, and squalor. Hesitatingly at first, the government began to set aside the policy of *laissez-faire* and legislation was passed to improve health and living conditions. Reformers must take the credit for persuading Parliament to pass these new laws. Other reformers, perhaps frustrated by the slowness of the government, tackled some of the problems themselves by building new and decent housing for their own workers or for the poor. Industrial Britain was very aware of the costs and profits of every enterprise. A powerful argument for improvement was the enormous cost of death and sickness. I. Gilchrist, a local town official, speaking to the Health of Towns Association in 1848, said:

Sickness is expensive by the cost of medical attendance, by loss of laborer's work and as causing premature death .... Think of 27,000 cases of widowhood, and 10,000 cases of orphanage arising from removable causes annually ... the annual cost of unnecessary sickness and death is £20,000,000 [about $100,000,000], all of which might be saved by proper sanitary measures.

Edwin Chadwick was the first civil servant who urged government action to improve people's health.

Creating Healthier Towns

In 1848, Parliament approved the first Public Health Act. Edwin Chadwick (1800–1890) played a prominent part in campaigning for this new law. Chadwick, as secretary of the Poor Law Commission, had investigated the link between poverty and health. If people suffered constant ill health, Chadwick argued, they were unable to work and became dependent on poor relief. It was in the interests of the government to promote good health to reduce the expense of funding the poorhouses where the really destitute were sent.

When reform was proposed, it was always strongly resisted by all kinds of vested interests. Landowners objected that they would have to pay for improvements. Water companies, builders, and landlords who profited from current arrangements were resistant to change of any kind. Well-off individuals, who feared an increased tax burden, clung to *laissez-faire* arguments.

The 1848 Public Health Act set up a Central Board of Health in London with the power to create local boards of health in towns where the death rate was exceptionally high. These boards were supposed to tackle cleaning, paving, and drainage of streets. Opposition to these boards was great and many towns chose to ignore the Act, no matter how bad conditions were. *The Times* newspaper called the 1848 Public Health Act,

Too often the water in cities was tainted and caused the spread of epidemics such as cholera. Even so, reform was resisted.

a reckless invasion of property and liberty.

Local authorities complained that Chadwick and the Board had interfered in their towns and tried to bully them into making expensive improvements. In 1854, opposition forced the Central Board to close. But by then, there was a growing awareness in local and central government that action and legislation were necessary. During the 1850s and 1860s, a number of Acts were passed aimed at tackling various problems. In London, the Metropolitan Board of Works was put in charge of the city's sewage and water supply. Sanitary and nuisance inspectors were authorized to examine lodging houses and, if necessary, get them cleaned up or closed down.

Eventually, in 1872 and 1875, two important Public Health Acts were passed. Under this legislation, local town councils were compelled to appoint sanitary inspectors, medical officers of health, and inspectors of nuisances. Each area had to provide at least one hospital. A little later, local councils were given the job of making sure that all food sold in their area was safe to be eaten. All of this meant that by the late 1870s, every part of the country had some kind of organization that was responsible for public health.

City streets were so filthy that well-off people paid a crossing sweeper to clear their path.

Better Homes for the Poor

Industrialization had resulted in many working-class families living in overcrowded and unhealthy homes. They were condemned to such properties unless their employer or a private charity provided for them. A few factory owners, such as Robert Owen, built good quality housing for their workers. In 1853, Titus Salt (1803–1876), a devout Christian, opened his new factory just outside Bradford. Besides providing good working conditions, he built the town of Saltaire for his workers to live in. The houses were some of the most spacious ever built for working-class people at that time. The town included a school, a hospital, and a Congregational Church. Many of the buildings remain in use today. As you entered the town, a notice read:

Abandon beer all ye who enter here.

Titus Salt, like many other reformers, was a supporter of the Temperance Movement and believed that alcoholic drinks such as beer and whisky ruined many working people's lives.

Titus Salt built decent homes for his workers, but what was really needed was government action to improve all working-class districts.

Philanthropic Efforts

Philanthropists such as George Peabody were generous with their wealth but were reluctant to allow working-class people to have political power.

Some poorer people benefited from the efforts of philanthropists, many of whom saw charity as their Christian duty. One of the first of these philanthropists was George Peabody (1795–1869), an American with a banking business in London. Between 1862 and 1866, he gave $725,000 (£145,000), an enormous sum at the time, to provide decent housing for the poor. Peabody's apartments had plenty of light and fresh air as well as modern washing and toilet facilities. Critics said they were too barracks-like with too many rules, but for many people it was their first dry, clean, and hygienic home. Even today, the Peabody Trust continues to provide decent housing for working-class families.

Octavia Hill (1838–1912) was one of the first women to take responsibility for managing

Homes of the London poor, 1854. The efforts of philanthropists were aimed at lifting the working-class out of poor housing conditions and their resultant problems.

working-class housing. She was convinced that it was bad housing that led to poor social behavior:

It is slums that make slum-dwellers, not slum-dwellers who make the slums.

She also thought that it was quite possible for landlords to provide decent standard housing and still make a reasonable profit. To prove her point, she borrowed some money from a friend and purchased some old tenements. She spent money on improving the property, including repairing the windows. She charged no more than a standard rent, but provided far superior accommodation that tenants began to take pride in for themselves. However, anyone who didn't pay the rent was quickly evicted.

Soap manufacturer W. H. Lever employed well-known architects to build Port Sunlight in Merseyside for his workers in 1888, with some homes in a mock-Tudor style.

The Changing Role of Government

The role of government changed very significantly during the 19th century. This was entirely in response to the problems spawned by industrialization and population growth. At the start of the 19th century, most members of the government perceived their job to be the protection of the nation from attack by a foreign enemy and the maintenance of law and order at home. The responsibility to set standards for life in towns and factories was not part of a government's mandate.

The extent of local government was mostly limited to the role of magistrates, who maintained law and order and administered some help to the poor. Any attempt at regulation was thought to challenge the rights of property owners, which were regarded as untouchable. The government, it was believed, did not have any right to tell people what they could or could not do with their own property. The highly regulated nature of modern-day society, with its multitude of legislation and government agencies, was alien to the 19th century.

Impressive town halls, such as this one in Manchester, symbolized the growth of local government in the late 1800s.

The Artisans' Dwelling Act of 1875 gave local authorities the power to clear slum districts like this London slum, photographed in 1900.

In the first half of the 19th century, even when the government did grant more powers to local authorities, it tended not make it compulsory for them to take action. It was not until after 1850 that local government grew considerably. By 1900, local town and city councils were responsible not only for public matters, such as sanitation and housing, but also for providing gas, water, and electric service.

The Rate of Reform

The rate of reform was slow—so slow and piecemeal that the bulk of slum housing was not dealt with until well into the 20th century. It was not until the bombing during World War II that some slums were demolished. At the beginning of the 19th century, the working class was deprived of the political power needed to effectively agitate for change. As the franchise (right to vote) was extended in the 19th century, political awareness of working-class needs also grew. There was a direct relationship between the extension of the franchise and the speed of reform.

The Number of Voters as a Proportion of the Adult Male Population

	England and Wales	Scotland	Ireland
1833	1 in 5	1 in 8	1 in 20
1869	1 in 3	1 in 3	1 in 6
1886	2 in 3	3 in 5	1 in 2

Only men were able to vote in parliamentary elections. However, female taxpayers (on local property) could vote in some local elections. The limiting of the franchise to taxpayers in local elections confirmed a natural tendency to keep the rates as low as possible. This discouraged local authorities from spending the necessary sums to tackle problems. Nevertheless, by 1900, an effective and professional system of local government was firmly in place.

Joseph Arch, a farm laborer and trade union leader, became the first working-class Member of Parliament in 1885.

CELEBRATION AND LEGACY

Celebrating the Machine Age

In the summer of 1851, thousands of people traveled to London to visit the Great Exhibition of the Works of Industry of All Nations. The driving force behind the exhibition was Queen Victoria's husband, Prince Albert. According to Prince Albert, the purpose of the exhibition was:

to present a true test and living picture of the point of development at which the whole of mankind has arrived and a new starting point, from which all nations will be able to direct their further exertions.

The exhibition, which was, in effect, a celebration of the Industrial Revolution, was an enormous success. It was housed in a huge glass building in Hyde Park, nicknamed by *Punch* magazine the "Crystal Palace." The structure contained 3,300 columns and 2,300 girders, with more than 984,252 feet (300,000 m) of glass. The exhibition attracted over six million visitors and, on its busiest day, saw 93,244 people attending. For many of the visitors, it was their first and perhaps only trip to London. The new railroads brought thousands down from the industrial cities of the North and the Midlands. The Queen, who opened the exhibition on May 1, was thrilled

by the beauty of the building and the vastness of it all.

Seven-thousand exhibitors filled the Crystal Palace to demonstrate Britain's industrial achievements.

Queen Victoria opened the exhibition. Organizing it was her husband's greatest achievement.

"The Most Beautiful Machinery"

Inside, the Crystal Palace was packed with displays from 7,351 British exhibitors and a further 6,556 from other countries. It was the British exhibits that attracted the most interest. Visitors were thrilled to see all kinds of steam-powered machinery as well as demonstrations of the new electric telegraph and a huge 39-foot (12-m) model of Liverpool Docks. Queen Victoria, writing in her journal after one of several visits to the Great Exhibition, remarked:

What used to be done by hand and used to take months doing is now accomplished in a few instants by the most beautiful machinery. We saw first the cotton machines from Oldham .... We saw hydraulic machines, pumps, filtering machines for purifying sugar—in fact, every conceivable invention.

The Great Exhibition was a demonstration of the enormous self-confidence of Victorian Britain. It showed off to everyone, including the rest of the world, British commercial and industrial supremacy. In every manufacturing industry, Britain led the way. In addition, most of the world's trade was carried by British ships. The vast British Empire, including India and huge areas of Africa, provided raw materials, ready markets, and good profits for British businesses.

The machinery court, with its hydraulic press and steam-driven machines, was the most popular part of the exhibition.

Britain in 1851

1851 was a good year to look back and take stock of what had been achieved and how the nation had changed. The previous hundred years had seen the Industrial Revolution bring sweeping changes and great national prosperity. In addition, Britain had avoided the political revolutions that had affected other European countries, such as France in 1789 and a number of countries in 1848, the "Year of Revolutions" (for example, Italy, Germany, France, and Switzerland). Britain enjoyed a relative degree of stability, law, and order, if not justice. Although people did not realize it, the Industrial Revolution had reached the peak of its achievement

Yet for all its self-satisfaction and national pride, Britain still had no effective legislation to tackle problems like public health and poor working conditions. Industrialization had created problems and also the means to solve most of them, but it had not produced the determination to deal with them. Many of the crowds who flocked to the Crystal Palace to be thrilled at Britain's progress returned home to slums and sweatshops. An immigrant girl to Australia declared in 1846:

I know what England is. Old England is a fine place for the rich, but the Lord help the poor.

Brunel's *Great Eastern* steamship could carry 4,000 passengers. In 1866, it laid a transatlantic telegraph cable linking the United States and Europe.

Growth in the United States

In the United States, rapid industrial expansion occurred after 1860. Pittsburgh was booming so as a manufacturing city that it was nicknamed the "Birmingham of America." A network of railroads opened up new markets for factories in the eastern states. During the Civil War, 1861–1865, industrial output concentrated on military equipment. After the war, large numbers of European immigrants provided millions of new workers and customers. The population more than doubled between 1860 and 1900, when it reached 76 million. Soon it was the Americans who were coming up with important new inventions. At the United States Centennial Exhibition of Arts, Manufactures, and Products of the Soil and Mine in Philadelphia in 1876, new products displayed included refrigerators, rotary printing presses, and the world's largest steam engine.

Alexander Graham Bell, an immigrant from Scotland, showed off his invention, the telephone. In 1860, 140,000 American manufacturing works turned out products worth $1.9 billion. By 1900, 207,000 manufacturing works produced goods valued at $11.4 billion. Although the U.S. still imported more goods than it sold overseas, that was about to change. During the 1890s, new foreign markets opened up in Canada, Asia, and South America.

Poverty and distress in Ireland, then ruled by Britain, drove millions of people to emigrate to the United States.

Alexander Graham Bell left Scotland for the United States, where he made his great invention, the telephone, in 1876.

A Changing World

Toward the end of the 19th century, as Britain was facing growing competition from other countries, we can say that the Industrial Revolution was over. Britain had entered the 19th century as the only industrialized nation, but by the 1880s, Britain's monopoly in developing new products and new methods of manufacture was finished. Industrial changes, now no longer revolutionary, were consolidating Britain as an industrial nation. An unexpected downturn in prices and profits in the 1880s was the first sign of difficulties. It was the beginning of a depression in which the economy, the production of goods, began to slow down. At the same time, growth in Germany and the United States increased. So worried were industrialists and politicians about the state of the economy that a Royal Commission on the Depression of Industry and Trade was set up in 1886. For the first time, the Commission drew attention to the threat posed by other countries, yet the spread of industrialization was unstoppable. By 1900, the U.S. was producing more coal and iron than Britain. Germany's iron output was also greater than Britain's. Japan, Sweden, and even Russia were making progress toward industrialization. Much of the machinery that launched these other industrial revolutions originated in Britain. Only Britain's textile industry remained unchallenged.

The Legacy

Visitors to the Great Exhibition could not foresee the changes ahead, and most of the adult visitors did not live to see them either. None of them had heard the term "Industrial Revolution," but they were well aware that their nation had changed. They expected further innovation, although the people of 1851 could not have imagined the direction inventiveness would take. Some of the children who visited the Crystal Palace lived long enough to see the arrival of the automobile, the telephone, electric light, and possibly the airplane. Benjamin Disraeli, prime minister in 1868 and 1874–1880, captured the belief and expectation of this generation:

Change is inevitable. In a progressive country, change is constant.

While there is a consensus that the Industrial Revolution was a major turning point, it brought a heady mixture of misery and success to those who lived through it. Undoubtedly, the material prosperity enjoyed today by Europeans and Americans has its origins in Britain's Industrial Revolution. Unfortunately, so do a myriad of the problems we face, including pollution, waste disposal, and over-consumption.

London's Strand in the 1890s. London's importance was soon to be challenged by Berlin and New York.

GLOSSARY

British Empire countries controlled by Britain. The Empire came to an end during the years after World War II.

broadcloth a fine woolen or worsted cloth made on a wide loom

capital money that is used to start up or improve a business with the idea of making a profit

cast iron heavy, strong, but very brittle iron, used to make parts of steam engines, machines, bridges, and buildings

colony a country owned and controlled by another country

cooperative movement a movement in which people work and trade together, with each person taking a fair share of the profit

direct action taking immediate action, such as sabotage, to get what you want

domestic system manufacturing goods, such as woolen cloth, in people's homes—the system used before the factory system

entrepreneur someone who sets up or expands a business by using capital, with the aim of making a profit

excrement human toilet waste

factory system system in which goods are made in factories using machinery

hand-loom weavers people who operated hand-powered machines to weave cloth

House of Commons the chamber of the British Parliament that is chosen by election

House of Lords the chamber of the British Parliament that is made up of members who have inherited their position or been awarded it by the monarch

industrialization the growth of industry on a very large scale

investment money that is put into a business with the expectation of making a profit

laissez-faire a French term used to describe the government policy of minimal interference in business and industry

martyr a person who suffers unfairly because of his or her beliefs

mass production manufacturing goods on a large scale using factory machinery, which means the goods are cheaper to make

navvies unskilled workers who built the canals and, later, roads and railways

patent a government grant to protect the rights of an owner of an invention

philanthropist a wealthy person who gives money to benefit other people

Radicals 19th-century politicians who campaigned for the working class to be allowed to vote and for social reforms that would benefit them

revolution a great political or social upheaval that leads to important changes. Political revolutions are often violent, such as those in France and Russia

socialist someone who believes in an equal distribution of wealth, good provision of welfare benefits, and the state ownership of industry

TIMELINE OF EVENTS

1712	Newcomen's steam engine.
1733	John Kay's flying shuttle.
1751	Start of "turnpike mania."
1761	The Bridgewater Canal between Worsley and Manchester opens.
1764	James Hargreaves invents the spinning jenny.
1766	James Brindley begins the Grand Trunk Canal project.
1769	Arkwright opens the first factory using the water frame.
1776	The thirteen American colonies declare their independence from Britain. James Watt's steam engine in use.
1779	Iron Bridge built at Coalbrookdale in Derbyshire.
1783	Britain recognizes the independence of the United States.
1784	Post office starts the first mail coach service.
1789	Start of the French Revolution.
1793	Beginning of Britain's wars with revolutionary France. In the U.S., Eli Whitney invents the cotton gin.
1799	First Combination Act
1800	Census population of the U.S., 5.3 million.
1801	First British census puts the population at 11.9 million.
1802	The *Charlotte Dundas*, the first successful steamship, launches.
1803	Richard Trevithick's *Catch Me Who Can* steam locomotive.
1807	First U.S. steamship, the *Clermont*, built by Robert Fulton.
1811	Start of Luddite machine-breaking.
1812	Start of two-year war with the U.S.
1814	Steam printing press used to print *The Times* newspaper.
1815	British victory at the Battle of Waterloo ends the wars with France. Davy's miner's safety lamp developed.
1816	Robert Owen opens the first school for factory children.
1825	George Stephenson completes the Stockton-to-Darlington railway line.
1830	Liverpool-to-Manchester railway line built by George and Robert Stephenson. In the U.S., South Carolina Railroad uses steam locomotives. Revolutionary political

movements in France, Germany, Poland, and Italy.

1832 First Parliamentary Reform Act extends the vote to many middle-class men.

1833 First Factory Act to restrict the working hours of women and children.

1834 Grand National Consolidated Trades Union.
Tolpuddle Martyrs.

1835 First use of the term "socialism."

1837 Start of the electric telegraph.
Victoria becomes Queen (until 1901).

1842 Chadwick reports on public health in towns.
Mines Act bans women and children from working underground.

1844 Start of "railway mania."
Rochdale cooperative Society set up.

1845 Maiden voyage of the first iron-built steamship, *Great Britain*.
Railway mania reaches a peak.

1847 Factory Act limits the working day for women and young people to ten hours.

1848 Revolutions in several European countries.

1851 The Great Exhibition.
New Model Trade Union set up to represent engineers.

1853 Titus Salt founds Saltaire.

1856 Bessemer converter.

1857 Steam power used to generate electric light.

1859 London Mains Drainage Scheme.

1861 Start of the U.S. Civil War (ended 1865).

1863 First part of London Underground Railway built.

1867 Parliamentary Reform Act extends the vote to some urban working-class men.

1870 Education Act introduces some compulsory schooling.

1876 Telephone demonstrated by Alexander Graham Bell in the U.S.

1878 First electric-floodlit football game in Sheffield.

1884 Internal combustion engine built by Daimler in Germany.
Parliamentary Reform Act extends the vote to some rural working-class men.

1888 London match-girls strike.

1889 London dockers strike.

1900 Labour Representation Committee (later called the Labour Party) established.
Census puts the population of the U.S. at 75.9 million.

1901 Census puts the population of Great Britain at 38.2 million.

BOOKS
TO READ

There are many excellent books on the Industrial Revolution. The following are especially useful:

Collins, Mary. *The Industrial Revolution (Cornerstones of Freedom)*. Danbury, CT: Children's Press, 2000.

Corrick, James A. *The Industrial Revolution (World History Series)*. San Diego, CA: Lucent Books, Inc., 1998.

Dudley, William. *The Industrial Revolution: Opposing Viewpoints (American History Series)*. San Diego, CA: Greenhaven Press, Inc., 1997.

Ingpen, Robert R. *The Industrial Revolution (Ideas That Changed the World)*. Broomall, PA: Chelsea House Publishers, 1995.

McCormick, Anita Louise. *The Industrial Revolution in American History (In American History)*. Berkeley Heights, NJ: Enslow Publishers, Inc., 1998.

Moss, Joyce. *Profiles in World History: Beginnings of the Age of Discovery to Industrial Revolution, Vol. 4*. Farmington Hills, MI: The Gale Group, 1995.

Wroble, Lisa A. *Kids During the Industrial Revolution (Kids Throughout History)*. New York: Rosen Publishing Group, 1999.

INDEX